ENGLISH EMBROIDERY—I

DOUBLE-RUNNING
OR
BACK-STITCH

By
LOUISA F. PESEL
Author of " Practical Canvas Embroidery " " Stitches from Old English Embroideries "
" Stitches from Eastern Embroideries " " Stitches from Western Embroideries "
" Leaves from my Embroidery Book."

WITH A PREFACE BY
MISS ETTA CAMPBELL
Teacher of Embroidery in the School of Art, Winchester

Embroidery

Embroidery is the handicraft of decorating fabric or other materials with needle and thread or yarn. Embroidery may also incorporate other materials such as metal strips, pearls, beads, quills, and sequins. An interesting characteristic of embroidery is that the basic techniques or stitches on surviving examples of the earliest patterns —chain stitch, buttonhole or blanket stitch, running stitch, satin stitch, cross stitch—remain the fundamental techniques of hand embroidery today.

In *The Art of Embroidery*, written in 1964 by Marie Schuette and Sigrid Muller-Christensen, they noted the 'striking fact that in the development of embroidery ... there are no changes of materials or techniques which can be felt or interpreted as advances from a primitive to a later, more refined stage. On the other hand, we often find in early works a technical accomplishment and high standard of craftsmanship rarely attained in later times.' Embroidery has been dated to the Warring States period in China (5th-3rd century BC). The process used to tailor, patch, mend and reinforce cloth fostered the development of sewing techniques, and the decorative possibilities of sewing led to the art of embroidery. Embroidery was also a very important art in the Medieval Islamic world. One of the most interesting accounts of the craft has been given by the seventeenth century Turkish traveller, Evliya Çelebi, who called it the 'craft of the two hands.'

Because embroidery was a sign of high social status in Muslim societies, it became a hugely popular art. In cities such as Damascus, Cairo and Istanbul, embroidery was visible on handkerchiefs, uniforms, flags, horse trappings, slippers, sheaths, covers, and even on leather belts; often utilising gold and silver thread. It has since spread to the rest of the world, particularly the UK, where professional workshops and guilds garnered an immense reputation. The output of these workshops, called *Opus Anglicanum* or 'English work', was famous throughout Europe.

Embroidery can be classified according to whether the design is stitched *on top of* or *through* the foundation fabric, and by the relationship of stitch placement to the fabric. Several important classifications include 'free embroidery', where designs are applied without regard to the weave of the underlying fabric (such as traditional Chinese and Japanese embroidery), 'Counted Thread embroidery' where patterns are created by making stitches over a predetermined number of threads in the foundation fabric, and 'Canvas Work', where threads are stitched through a fabric mesh to create a dense pattern that completely covers the foundation fabric. This can be done on almost any fabric; wool, linen and silk have been in use for thousands of years, although today - cotton, ribbons, and organza are frequently utilised.

Whilst there is now a burgeoning market for commercial embroidery, and much contemporary embroidery is stitched with a computer using digital patterns, the art and pleasure of embroidery as a craft is making a comeback. We hope that the reader is inspired by this book to try some of their own!

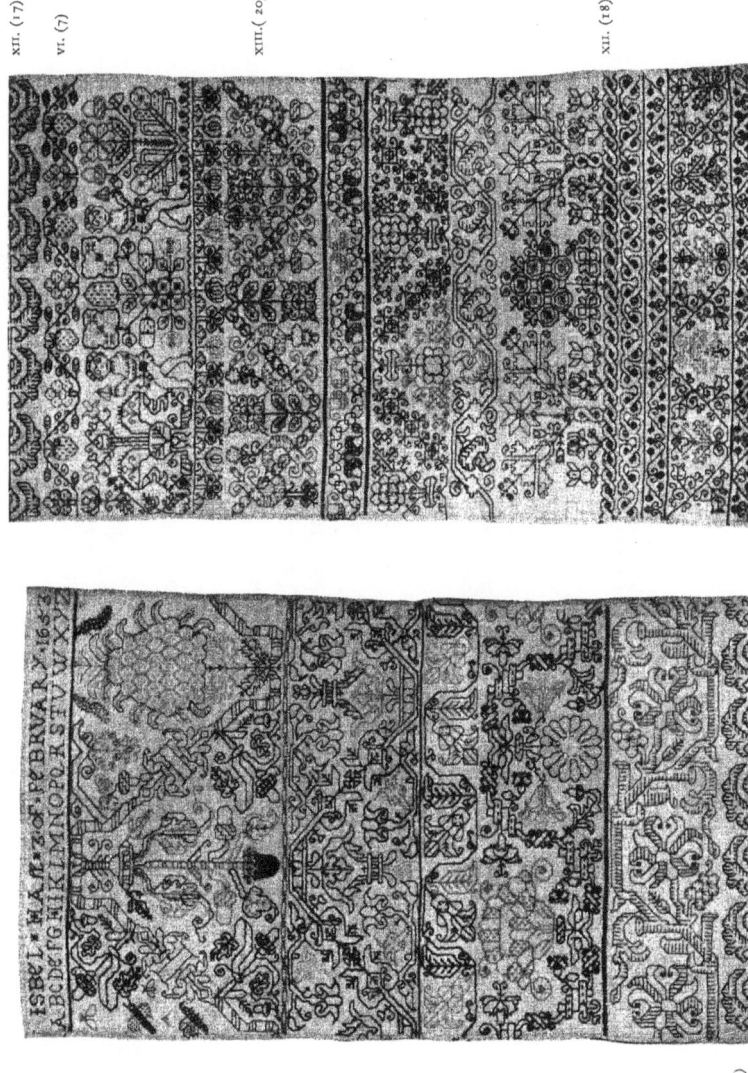

SEVENTEENTH-CENTURY ENGLISH SAMPLER WORKED BY ISBEL HALL, FEBRUARY 1633. *Now in the possession of Mrs. CLEMENT WILLIAMS.*

The designs are very varied, and are worked in double running. Emphasis is given by eyelet holes, and in some places the flowers and leaves have a darned surface. Some of the designs are amongst the diagrams worked out to scale.

The numbers at the sides indicate the Plate references on which diagrams will be found showing the practical working of the stitches.

PREFACE

I WAS very glad when I was asked to write the Preface for this book, because I look upon it as an honour to be associated with the publication of a book written for the purpose of bringing back English tradition and designs for our Embroideries. Too often we forget these traditions and designs, and we model our work on foreign types, not altogether fitted to our temperament.

I especially welcome this book, which will make it easy to study and copy authentic English designs. I know how extremely useful it will prove with its photographs and charts. Possibly very few people realize the endless patience necessary for making these copies from old samplers, since the minutest details must be faithfully reproduced to ensure the perfect accuracy of the complete design, and many workers will be grateful to Miss Pesel for providing these charts, which will be found quite easy to use in numerous ways. To my mind Double-Running does not lend itself very readily to modern ideas, and I should strongly advise all who wish to learn this type of work to begin by copying these early designs, and later to make selections from them to suit their individual requirements.

There is another aspect which is not always realized in this work done by the counted thread, and that is its value in regard to health. The work needs sufficient concentration to keep the mind occupied without undue strain, and I have proved by experience with my pupils the worth of this. After a short time spent in working at a design, very often the obvious weariness following a long day in school or office will disappear. In these days of rush and hurry, I believe half an hour each day spent in embroidery of this type would act as a real tonic, and, in addition, workers would have the satisfaction of knowing that they were helping to establish once more in this country the old designs made and worked by their ancestresses many years ago.

ETTA CAMPBELL,
Teacher of Embroidery, Winchester School of Art.

TWYFORD, WINCHESTER,
February 1931.

ACKNOWLEDGMENTS

THANKS.

THE owners of precious old English samplers have again allowed me to make drawings from their treasures, and so have made this book possible.

My thanks for permission to use their samplers are due to the authorities of the Victoria and Albert Museum. To Mrs. Clement Williams, who is the possessor of the beautiful dated sampler used as a coloured frontispiece. To Miss Ravenhill for drawings from a sampler she had copied long ago. To Professor Newberry, for the old Egyptian sampler illustrated here to show how, long ago, line work in double running was in fashion. To the Embroiderers' Guild for a sampler from the collection of embroideries loaned to them by Lady Egerton. To various friends for permission to photograph modern specimens worked by the Yew Tree Industry, and inserted here to show the effect of these designs when actually worked.

Our thanks, the reader's and mine, are certainly due to the photographers who have, with such infinite pains, succeeded in giving us the effect of the samplers—a most difficult feat, as the backgrounds have changed and the colours are often so faded that the values seem to disappear.

My personal thanks are also due to many unknown readers who have given my previous Embroidery books such a warm and friendly reception.

CONTENTS & LIST OF PLATES

FRONTISPIECE. 17th-Century English Sampler. Worked by Isbel Hall, 1635. Belonging to Mrs. Clement Williams.

                                                              PAGE

PREFACE, by Etta Campbell, Teacher of Embroidery at the School of Art, Winchester   7

ACKNOWLEDGMENTS 9

Plate   I. Sampler from Egypt, belonging to Prof. P. Newberry.

Plate   II. Top portion of English Sampler. Dated 1661. 368–1907, V. & A. M.

INTRODUCTION, by Louisa F. Pesel 15

Plate   III. Lower portion of Plate II.

Plate   IV. English Cross-Stitch and Double-Running Sampler, from the Collection of Lady Egerton.

Plate   V. Diagrams, from a Sampler belonging to Mrs. Clement Williams.

Plate   VI. Diagrams, from Sampler belonging to Mrs. Clement Williams, from one in the possession of the Author, and from No. 516, 1877, V. & A. M.

Plate   VII. A 17th-Century Sampler in the possession of the Author.

Plate   VIII. English Sampler from Mrs. C. Williams' Collection.

Plate   IX. Modern Reproduction by the Yew Tree Industry of Design on Plate VIII.

Plate   X. Modern Reproductions by Yew Tree Industry.

Plate XI. Diagrams, from Sampler by Isbel Hall, dated 1653, belonging to Mrs. Clement Williams, and from Sampler which belonged to the late Canon Greenwell.

Plate XII. Diagrams from some of Mrs. C. Williams' Samplers and from the late Canon Greenwell's Sampler and one of the Author's.

Plate XIII. Diagrams from 751–1902 and another, V. & A. M.

Plate XIV. Diagrams from 751–1902 and another, V. & A. M.

Plate XV. Diagrams from Samplers belonging to Mrs. Clement Williams, Miss Ravenhill, and the Author.

Plates XVI, XVII, and XVIII. Adapted from Samplers belonging to Mrs. Williams and from Designs in an old Pattern Book.

PLATE I.

COPTIC SAMPLER FROM EGYPT
Probably one of the oldest "Double-Run" Samplers known.

In the possession of Prof. P. NEWBERRY.

ENGLISH SAMPLER (Top Portion). For Lower Portion see Plate III.
Linen, embroidered with coloured silks in various stitches, including cross and satin stitch, and knotted stitches. Dated 1661.
(Size 36¼ inches by 11 inches)

1. *See* Diagram, *English Embroidery—Cross-Stitch*, Plate XIV. 22. VICTORIA AND ALBERT MUSEUM, 368-1907.
2. *See* Diagram, *English Embroidery—Cross-Stitch*, Plate XV. 27.
See also *Leaves from my Embroidery Note-Books*.

INTRODUCTION

IT is an evident fact that Handicrafts, and Embroidery in particular, have come to take an important place in modern life. A distinct revival in the interest in all crafts is noticeable in all countries, and is certainly marked in the British Isles.

It is interesting that this should have come at a time when all mechanical production has reached such a high state of perfection. It rather suggests that there is a quite irradicable need in us to do some work with our hands. Now that machinery has taken the place of the hand in the making of so many articles in common daily use, mankind evidently still feels the necessity for an outlet for the urge to construct some object with his hands that shall satisfy his universal longing for beauty. If a study is made of the objects of utility constructed in ancient times by the most primitive races, it is seen that early in advancing civilization the workers begin to decorate the objects they make. They appear to feel that they must add beauty to usefulness. This longing for things beautiful has persisted to our times, and is still active in many of us to-day.

Just where does British work, British needlework—for it is with that that we are occupied here—stand in this revival? Are we going to take our place as leaders at the top of the tree, or are we going to be content to follow in the wake of other countries? In the thirteenth century English embroideries were world-famed; and, personally, I do not see any reason why we should not recapture that reputation. In order to build up a school of work that is national in character and different in style from what is done in other countries, we should base our new work on our own best traditional types, and quite definitely and consciously develop on our own lines. This is what is being done to-day in Italy, Denmark, Poland, and Jugo-Slavia, to mention only a few countries. Recently a friend brought me a small handbook from Italy, giving descriptions of some two dozen different types of embroidery which are being revived there. When I was in Denmark last year I saw the work they were doing in their various schools of embroidery. In each of them they have collected many specimens of their beautiful linen stitchery. "Hedebo," it is called, and they are reviving work based on these wonderful old models. They are also using their old peasant dresses as models for their coloured embroidery. If other countries are doing this, should

LINE WORK IN DOUBLE - RUN - NING OR BACK - STITCH.

LINE WORK IN
DOUBLE-RUNNING
OR BACK - STITCH
continued.

we not be wise to do so also? Visitors wish to buy what is typical of a country, not copies of foreign work, and certainly our fellow-countrywomen, when they return home from the Dominions and Colonies, would like to take back with them things that are suggestive of or at least reminiscent of the old country. It is obvious, therefore, that if our embroidery were again to become a national industry, it would have a greater chance of being successful if it were markedly British in character.

Those who have studied our embroideries in the Victoria and Albert Museum, in loan exhibitions, and in private collections, realize that we possess most beautiful models to work from if we will only use them properly. They will give us a sounder lead than any work produced by foreigners can possibly do, because they were originally worked by our forbears.

It is interesting to find how general innate good craftsmanship is in many of our people, once it is aroused and trained. It has only been lying dormant, and a very little urging seems to revive it. I know this is true from personal experience, as I am sure many other teachers do. Here, in this village, in only four years, many previously inexperienced workers have developed into skilled and expert workers of linen embroidery, both white work and double running. They now do work that can compare favourably with some of the finest old work of the same type. Another group of workers in canvas embroidery, also without experience, have turned out a set of chair-seats, cushions, and kneelers for the private chapel at Wolvesey, which are a real achievement, for in every case the balancing of colour was their own. The designs were all adapted from old English seventeenth-century samplers, and that was, I think, probably the reason that they received so much praise, and incidentally a gold star, when they were seen at the exhibition of the National Federation of Women's Institutes. They were so typically English in feeling, design, and colour.

Some two years ago the Handicrafts Committee of the Hampshire County Federation of Women's Institutes decided to specialize in linen and canvas embroidery, and a number of its members went into these subjects rather fully. I prepared many designs from the old seventeenth-century samplers. Once these designs had been worked out to scale, on squared paper, it seemed a pity to keep them for ourselves. It is some of these designs which I propose now to publish, with descriptions and details, so as to make them available for use by a larger circle of workers.

Although the designs in this volume are mostly from double-run patterns, they can be used with modifications and other stitches to give other effects, and this is where the clever worker has her chance to show and develop her own skill and originality of treatment.

PLATE III.

ENGLISH SAMPLER (Lower Portion)
For top portion see Plate II.

UPPER HALF

LOWER HALF

ENGLISH SAMPLER
(Size 15 inches by 6 inches)

In the Collection of LADY EGERTON

MOST of the designs illustrated come from seventeenth-century samplers, many of them in the Victoria and Albert Museum, some from private collections. Two of the samplers are dated 1643 and 1653. It is interesting that they should have been worked and dated at a time when Cromwell and the Puritans had been destroying and condemning all things beautiful, and one wonders if, by chance, some of them were secretly worked by women or girls who were anxious to keep a record of their precious embroideries, if the originals should suffer destruction.

THE SOURCE OF DESIGNS.

THE actual origin of many of these designs is uncertain. It is possible that the more formal ones were influenced by pattern books from Italy, but the majority differ from those found on existing Italian specimens, as they have a distinct character of their own. It will be seen that flowers are generally introduced, and this rather points to their English origin, as the use of flowers is a marked characteristic of nearly all types of English embroidery. In Italy strange beasts and birds are often introduced.

THEIR ORIGIN

Given a certain number of these typical designs, it should be possible to build up an increasingly large and varied group of work, as each individual worker adds to it by using her own adaptations and modifications. A design could be copied on a larger scale, and then filled in with quite a different variety of stitch, and the final result would be only remotely reminiscent of the original design. A pattern worked in monochrome and a diversity of stitches would look totally different to the same design embroidered in colours and only a few stitches. Portions might be taken from several designs and combined for some special purpose, so long as the parts are in the right relation to each other as to treatment and scale.

THIS type of design, when it comes from Italy, is usually worked only in one colour, which is most often a deep blood red. On the English samplers the designs are often worked in one colour, but it varies; sometimes it is blue, or maybe a soft red, or a wine colour, a green, or shrimp pink. Some designs are, however, worked in several colours: red, green, and blue; or green, two blues, red, and yellow.

COLOUR.

WE shall never know for what objects these designs were originally intended, as they are not found on any existing embroideries. This fact suggests that they were meant for the decoration of household linen, cushions, covers, etc.—things that would be subjected to washing and hard wear, and not being considered important works of art, only just domestic

USE.

objects for everyday use, they would be discarded and thrown away when fashion changed or they were worn out. They are, however, designs that are very suitable for such domestic use in a present-day ménage.

MATERIALS.

THESE designs are undoubtedly best worked on an open linen, woven with a round thread, as on such a linen the stitches can be counted easily. Some of the linens made to-day are pressed very flat—" beetling," it is called—and thus makes a smooth and close surface on which the threads are much less clearly seen. Such linens are not really satisfactory, and make this double-running embroidery difficult, whilst on the right background it is easy and pleasant to work.

The thread with which they are best worked depends upon the use to which the finished embroidery is to be put and the fineness of the required result. The twisted D.M.C. coton perlé gives good results, either No. 5, 8, or 12—No. 12 being the finest for use on the finer linens. Washing Filoselle is useful for really fine work, and, in black, gives a result like a print.

NEEDLES.

THERE is less risk of splitting the threads of the linen background if a blunt-pointed needle is used, and incidentally it is much less damaging to the worker's first finger.

SCALE.

THE beginner will be wise to start by working three threads to the square, because threes are much easier to count. If a design seems to be too big in scale it can either be worked on a finer linen or worked over two threads to the square, which, of course, reduces it by one-third.

On some of the original pieces the borders are smaller than they are drawn in these diagrams, because whilst the wide centre border is done over three threads, the marginal borders are over two threads only.

DETAILS OF TECHNIQUE.

IT is a matter of purely personal choice whether these line patterns are carried out in double-running or back-stitch. The former, if properly worked, gives a back as neat as the front, and this is in its favour. The secret of a tidy wrong side is simple, once the principle of travelling is mastered. The first few repeats of a new pattern need attention, after which it becomes automatic and pleasant to do. The small diagram will make the method clear.

Start at A, travelling over three threads under three threads alternately, whether it is on the straight or across the diagonal of a square. The pattern for the wave is four diagonals downwards, two straight stitches, four diagonals upwards, and two straight, and so on for

PLATE V.

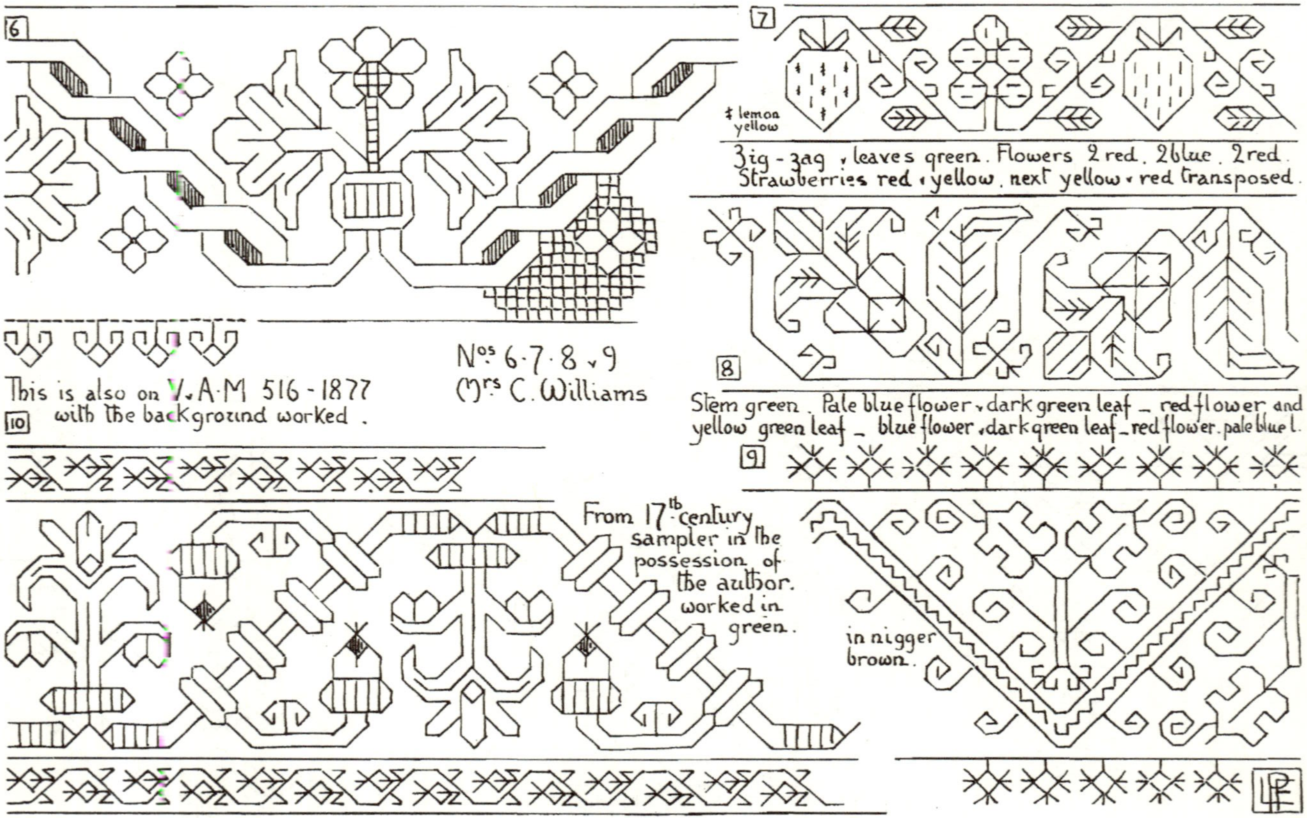

PLATE VI

[6]

[7]

½ lemon yellow

Zig-zag ; leaves green. Flowers 2 red. 2 blue. 2 red. Strawberries red , yellow. next yellow , red transposed.

[8]

Stem green. Pale blue flower, dark green leaf – red flower and yellow green leaf – blue flower, dark green leaf – red flower, pale blue l.

[9]

in nigger brown.

Nos 6.7.8.9
Mrs C. Williams

This is also on V.A.M 516-1877 with the background worked.

[10]

From 17th century sampler in the possession of the author. worked in green.

PLATE VII.

xv. (27)

xii. (14)

vi. (10)

xii. (13)

xv. (26)

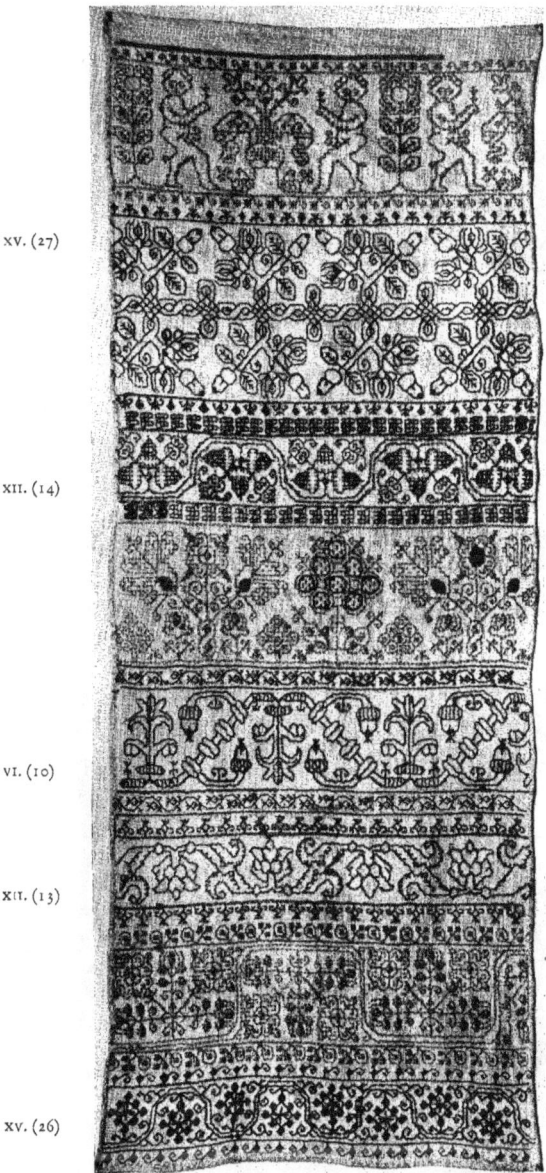

ENGLISH SAMPLER, SEVENTEENTH CENTURY
The numbers at the side indicate the Plate references on which diagrams will be found showing the practical working of the stitches.

In the possession of THE AUTHOR.

UPPER HALF

LOWER HALF

ENGLISH SAMPLER
(Size 14¾ inches by 8½ inches)
The numbers at the sides indicate the Plate references on which diagrams will be found showing the practical working of the stitches.

In the possession of Mrs. CLEMENT WILLIAMS.

DETAILS OF TECHNIQUE *continued.*

the length required. At B, turn and retrace to fill up the gaps that were left uncovered on the outward journey. At C, leave the wave to work the detail, over, under, round the outside edge of the triangular shape. At D, turn and retrace, doubling back on the stitches until E is reached, then put in the lines right and left, and then proceed. Arriving again at C, putting the needle in from above and coming out at F, the thread is in position to continue the wave until another detail or some offshoot has to be made. The small spike each side of the line can be worked either on the outward or on the return journey.

It is the turning back and retracing that is important, and at first it is difficult to remember not to stretch vaguely with a long stitch across the back, for that is what leads to trouble and an untidy wrong side.

In working the return journey always put the needle in at the top corner of the stitch worked on the previous journey, and come out at the lower corner—this detail sounds an unimportant one, but in the actual working it will be found to give a much better line.

The neatest way of beginning and ending off the thread is to run it in, on the right side, over one thread, under one thread, over, say, six or eight threads. The pattern then comes over it, and it is not seen, and makes a wrong side which is quite as tidy as the right. Though the condition of the reverse side does not matter, say, for a cushion, it is very important for table mats, as it sometimes happens that they are placed wrong side up. If the back is really tidy, this mistake is of no matter—only a compliment to the worker.

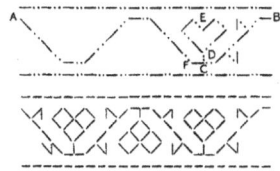

DETAILS OF TECHNIQUE *continued.*

So much for the actual technique. The only remaining point is the advice to consider carefully the proportion of the borders in relation to the size of the article to be worked, and the relation of the worked portions to the linen left plain. For example, on a long runner broad borders would certainly look well across each end. It is then generally necessary to run a narrow edging border along the long sides to link up the embroidery at the ends. Sometimes a small detail placed in the centre adds to the balance.

At first the novice is glad of all or any hints, but she will soon discover for herself just how wide to make her borders and hems, and where to put extra decoration, because she needs more weight to balance the whole. She will begin by designing corners, which she needs to turn her pattern, then she will plan a centre detail composed of elements in her design, and so little by little she will gain confidence and find herself making her own designs; and then we in England will find we have developed a style of our own, just faintly reminiscent of the old designs in this book.

LOUISA F. PESEL.

TWYFORD,
Spring, 1931.

DETAILS ABOUT SOME OF THE DIAGRAMS

PLATE II.
No. 6.—On Mrs. Williams's sampler this design is in outline, and has the small border at each edge, whilst on the museum sampler the background is all worked in blue in line stitch, with the result that the pattern stands out in white, on the darker background.

PLATE III.
Nos. 11 and 12 are designs which could be worked with a thicker outline, and have pulled stitches and damask stitches used as fillings within the various shapes.

PLATE IV.
No. 15 could be worked as suggested for Nos. 11 and 12.

PLATE VII.
No. 26.—These diamond-shaped flowers could be worked as eyelet holes, still keeping the diamond, if a heavier result was required.

PLATES VIII., IX., AND X.
These three sheets give designs which would be suitable for long narrow cushions about 26 in. wide and 14 in. deep, or for the ends of a long runner or sideboard cloth, or for large workbags. If used for a table centre or runner, the small designs could be arranged as a border for matching table mats.
These three are good for a fine effect worked in Filoselle silk.

PLATE IX.
No. 35.—Two alternatives are given, as the same design could be used with either a lighter or a heavier framework, according to the use for which it is required.

A Modern Reproduction of Plate VIII. by Yew Tree Industry
(See Plate VII.)
(For Diagram, see Plate XV.)

PLATE X.

MODERN WORK BY YEW TREE INDUSTRY, TWYFORD, HANTS.
Table Runners and Mats

MATERIALS . . D.M.C. cottons and linen backgrounds.
COLOURS . . (A) Red and green ; (B) Red, green, and blue.
STITCHES . . Double-running.
DESIGNS . . . From Old English Seventeenth-Century Samplers.
(For Diagrams see Plates XIII. and XIV.)

PLATE XI.

11. From an English sampler worked by Isabel Hall, dated 1653, belonging to (?) Clement Williams.

12. From a black-work sampler formerly in the possession of the late Canon Greenwell.

PLATE XII.

Nos 13, 14 are from a 17th century sampler belonging to the author.

From an all black-work sampler formerly in the possession of the late Canon Greenwell.

Nos 16, 17 & 18 Mrs C. Williams.

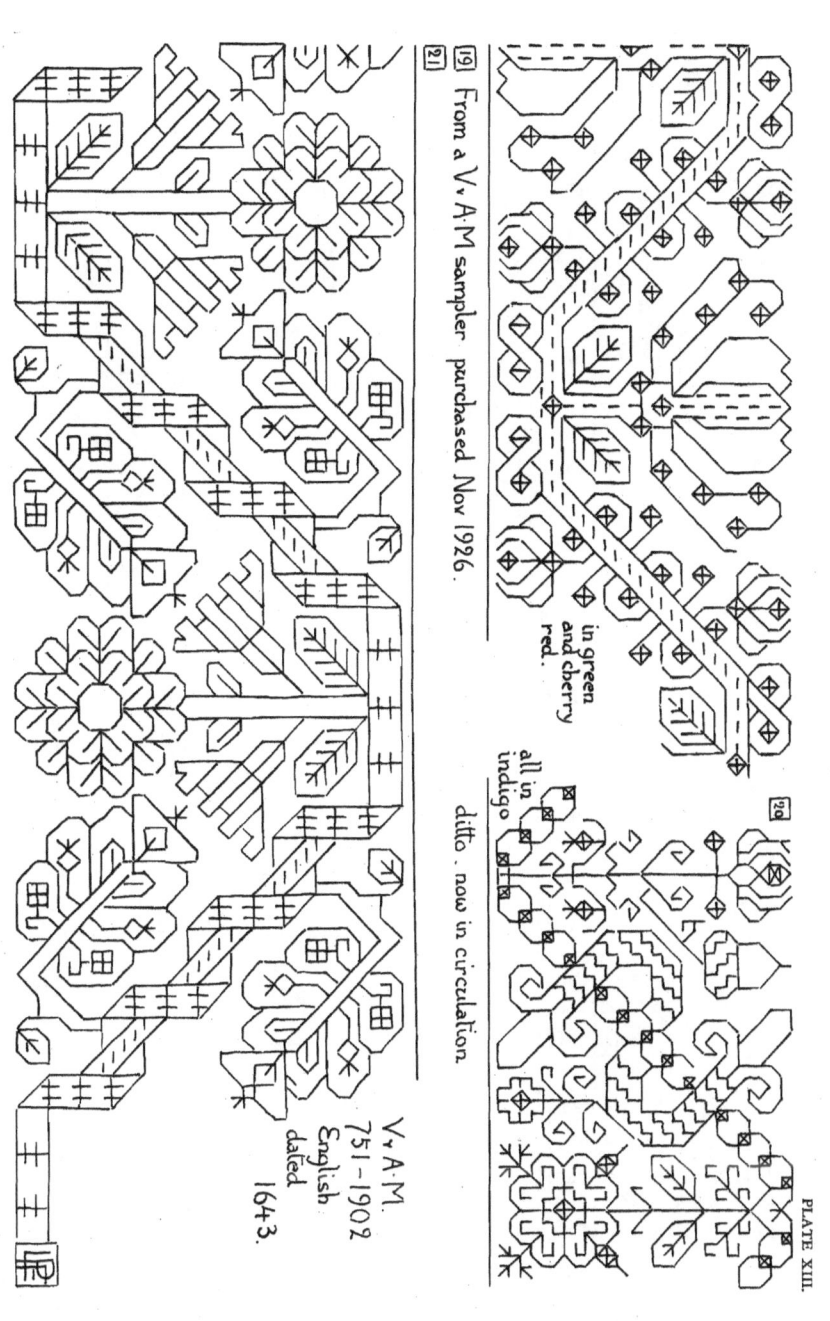

PLATE XIII.

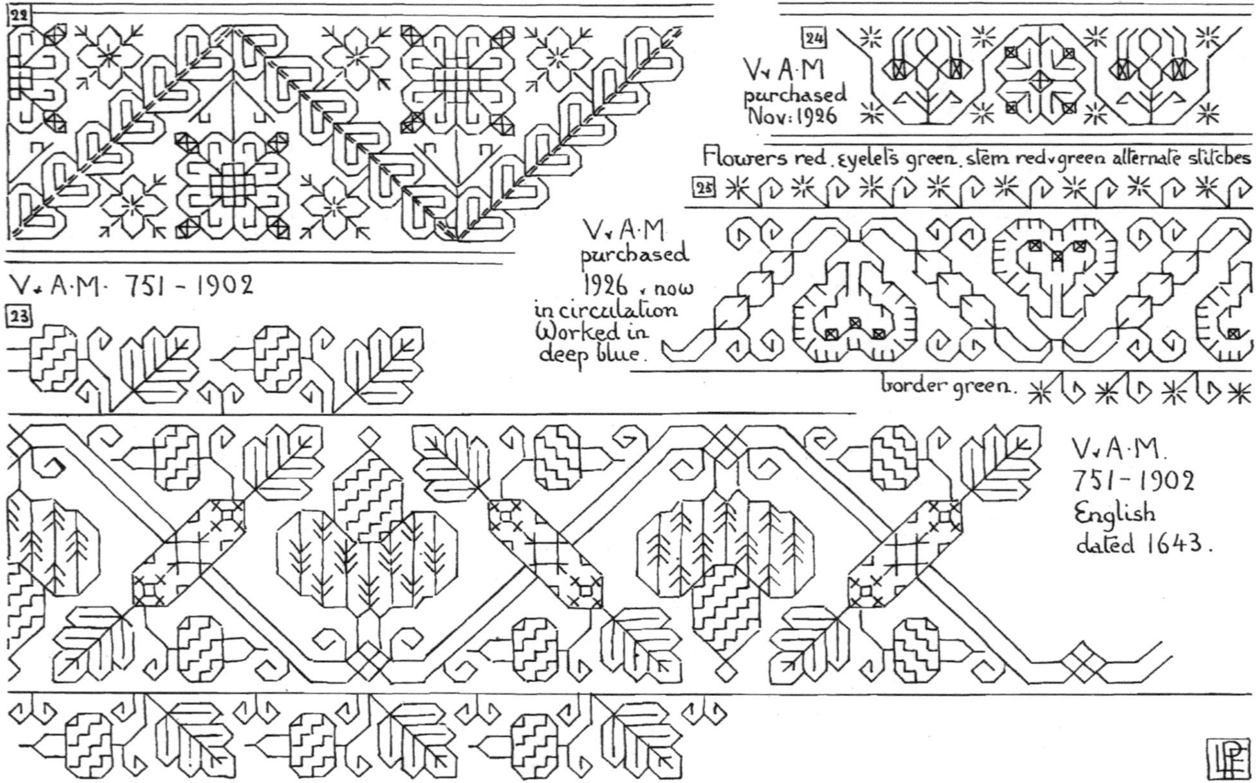

PLATE XIV.

[22]

[24] V.A.M purchased Nov: 1926

Flowers red. Eyelets green. stem red+green alternate stitches

[25] V.A.M purchased 1926, now in circulation Worked in deep blue.

border green.

V.A.M. 751-1902

[23] V.A.M. 751-1902 English dated 1643.

PLATE XV.

PLATE XVI.

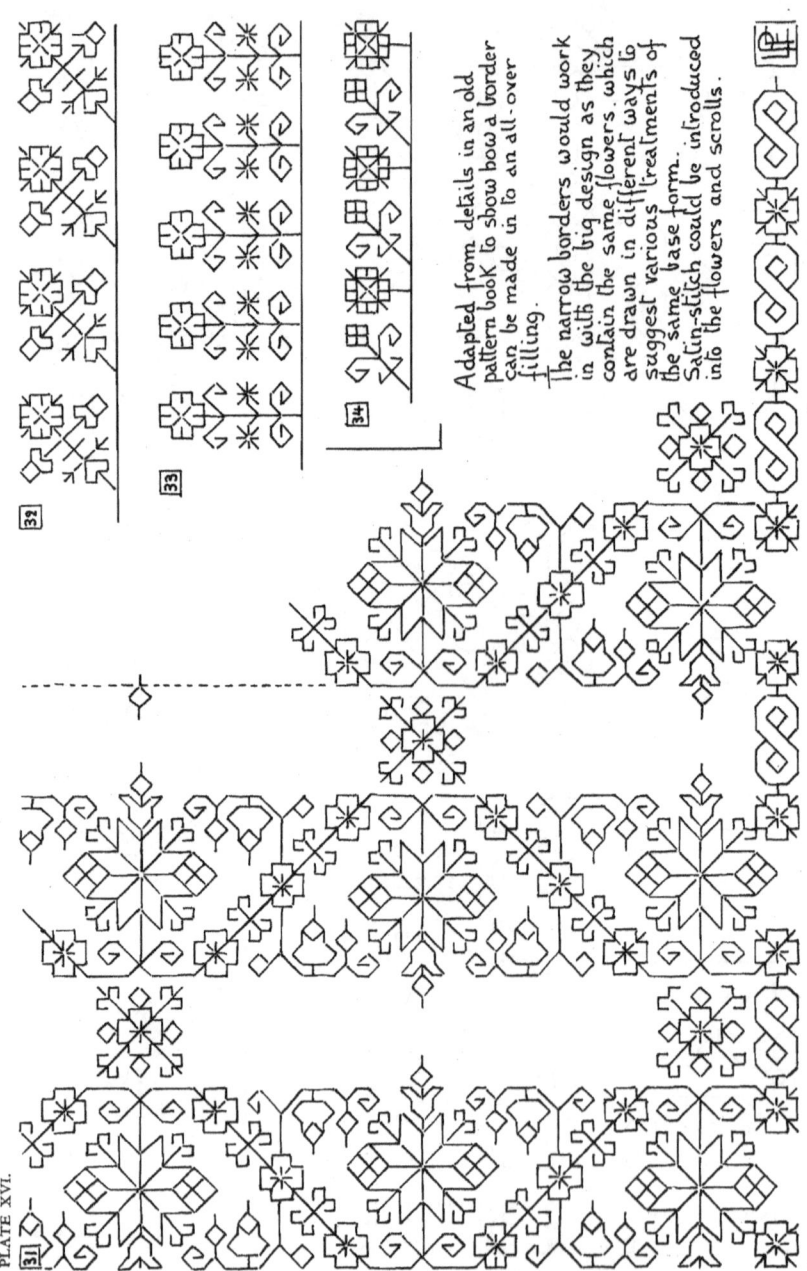

Adapted from details in an old pattern book to show how a border can be made in to an all-over filling.

The narrow borders would work in with the big design as they contain the same flowers, which are drawn in different ways to suggest various treatments of the same base form.

Satin-stitch could be introduced into the flowers and scrolls.

PLATE XVII.

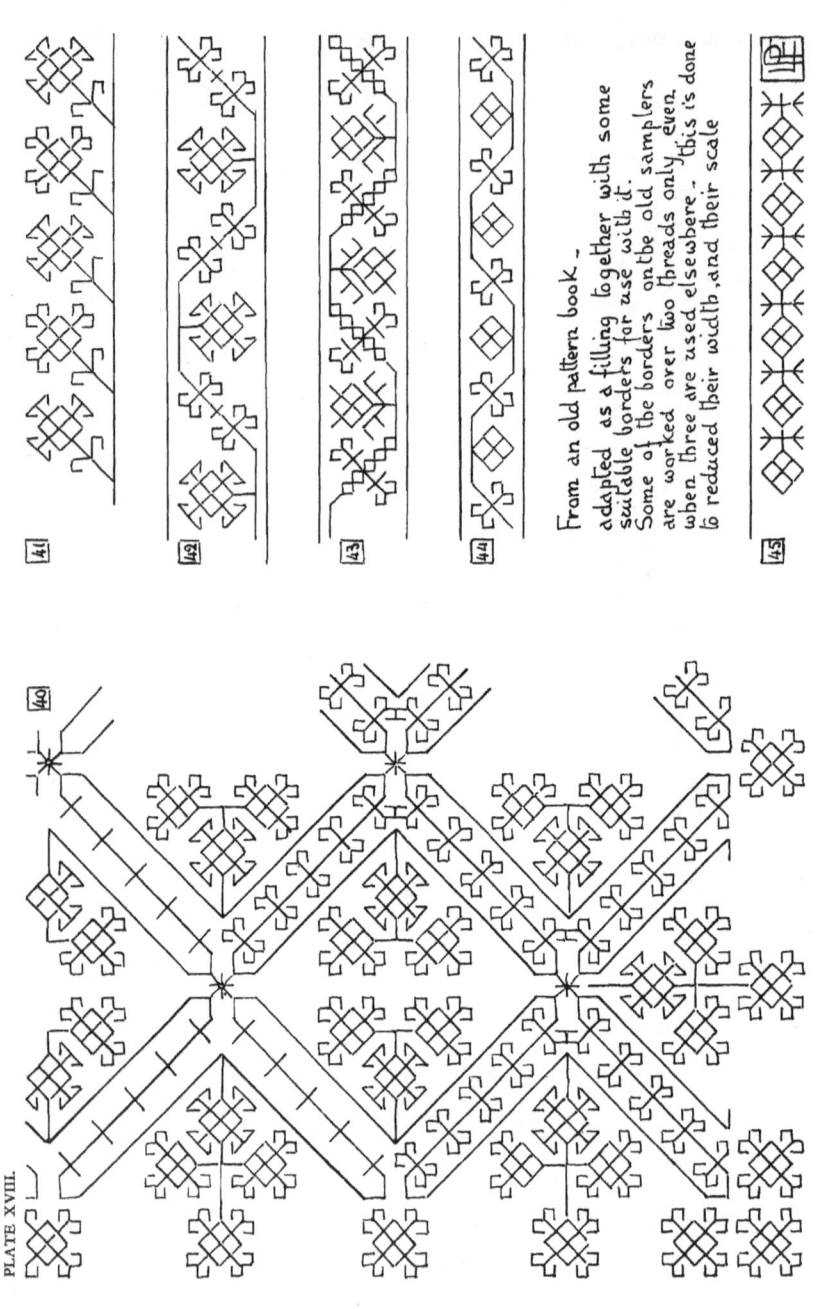

PLATE XVIII.

41
42
43
44

From an old pattern book — adapted as a filling together with some suitable borders for use with it. Some of the borders on the old samplers are worked over two threads only, even when three are used elsewhere. this is done to reduce their width, and their scale

45
46

NOTES

NOTES

www.ingramcontent.com/pod-product-compliance
Lightning Source LLC
Chambersburg PA
CBHW022125090426
42743CB00008B/1014